UNOFFICIAL

AMONG US
DIARY OF A CREWMATE

Prequel
Red Diary

Kid-Fi Media

Table of Contents

Red Data Log, Entry #1
Life as a Newbie Crew Member

Red here. It's been a pretty hectic past few days. I've been trying to get familiar with the spaceship since I got here. Being the newest crew member of the Gos, it's been a lot to take in.

There are a lot of rooms to understand and familiarize yourself with. The Gos is cutting-edge when it comes to technology, too, so this isn't like learning how to ride a bike. Nah, it's a lot more complicated than that.

There are a lot of machines, and I don't know what most of them even do. I only just figured out how to boil water and flush the toilet.

They've assigned me a trainer, Brown. Brown's been pretty nice so far. He's demanding but fair.

If you're wondering why I'm "Red" instead of "Noob," we all go by code names depending on the colors of our spacesuits. Red is a great color too, though I look like a giant tomato with arms and legs. And some of us even have pets on board! Pretty cool, right? It's pretty awesome for a rookie crew member like myself. Like I said before, a lot to take in, but I'm managing.

Keeping an electronic diary helps keep me grounded, so I can cope better. Brown was the one who recommended I keep a diary. It's a common practice among all the crew members, and it's all encrypted, so no one can read anyone else's entries. It was a shame—I loved reading diaries, especially my sister's.

Today, Brown's going to show me more stuff around the Gos. The ship is absolutely huge, and there are a ton of tasks to do—the fun and work never end!

Brown Data Log, Entry #1
More Lessons

Today, I'm going to show Red around the ship a little bit more. I have to admit it's pretty fun teaching a wide-eyed kid like Red. He has so much enthusiasm and excitement. He reminds me of myself when I was a new crew member. He absorbs knowledge like a sponge. He also looks like a big tomato. I don't want to say what I look like in my brown spacesuit.

Blue's pet came walking down the hall just now. I already told Blue to keep that dog on a leash. I'm not cleaning up after him. That's supposed to be a job for Blue. If you ask me, the Gos' regulations on pets are way too lax. This is a spacecraft, and we have cats, dogs and even a small alien on board as pets! Sometimes the dogs follow me. Maybe they think I'm a big piece of chocolate in my spacesuit. Or maybe it's because I like to keep sausages in my pocket.

But we have to maintain some kind of order around here! Oh, well. I guess I'll have to be the one to go get that dog again. When I catch up to him, I'm going to really give Blue a piece of my mind!

Red Data Log, Entry #2

A Helping Hand

Brown showed me around the ship's lobby today. There's a nice little couch in the middle and a large flat-screen monitor, plus a panel in front and what looked like a gamepad. The whole setup looked like a gamer's room. This ship was getting cooler and cooler by the minute! I always dreamed of having a gamer's room, a place to just play games and eat pizza at the same time (yeah, that's how good I am at gaming!).

"I like this room! Really cool!" I said.

Brown nodded.

"I had a feeling you would like the meteor room!" he said, and I could tell he was smiling behind his helmet.

"Meteor room? That's what this is?" I asked. Brown nodded again.

"Yep. Take a seat on the couch and let me explain."

I lowered myself onto the wide couch. It was really comfortable. Brown sat beside me and took the gamepad.

"You see, we're traveling through space, and that brings unique risks. One of those risks is slamming into some meteors. You can see them on the monitor, right?"

I looked at the screen and saw what Brown was talking about. The asteroids were right there in high definition. Staring at their projections on the screen, I was in awe. The meteors looked so huge and scary. I don't want the ship to slam into any of those things, that's for sure!

"Of course, no one wants to collide with those huge rocks. So we set up this meteor room like a game room. This way, blasting the meteors is easy and fun!"

"Ooh! Lemme try! Lemme try!"

I gushed like a little kid as Brown handed me the gamepad. I took one look at the screen and started blasting away at several meteors. Brown didn't even have to teach me anything! Everything came naturally.

"Looks like you're a natural at this stuff!" he said. "I think you're going to ace this task."

"You bet! I love to play video games!"

"So you spend a lot of time playing video games?!" asked Brown.

"Oh, yes! It's my favorite hobby after cake decorating!"

"I love cake!" said Brown, visibly excited.

"Everyone loves cake; it's the best thing ever. And you know what?"

"What?" asked Brown.

"You can eat a whole birthday cake even if it is not your birthday!"

He nodded in wonder.

The thought of cake almost distracted us from the several meteors that came into view, but I blasted all of them because I am just plain awesome. I could have spent the entire day in the meteor room.

Just then, the alarm went off. A loud siren echoed throughout the ship. The lights blinked on and off with a red hue.

"What happened?" I asked.

As if to answer my question, a voice blared, "Emergency in the O2 room! Emergency! Oxygen tanks have been tampered with! Oxygen tanks need to be repaired immediately. Ship is now running on reserve oxygen."

That didn't sound good at all. The ship had an artificial atmosphere and air supply so we could here without choking. If the O2 room ever got permanently damaged, we wouldn't have air to breathe.

"Well, you heard that, Red. O2 room's been compromised!" Brown said.

"Yeah, but how could that happen? I mean, in the briefings, I was told the Gos was, like, cutting-edge. Stuff here's gone through so many stress tests! Green handles maintenance, and we all know how strict and meticulous he is. How could something happen in the O2 room?"

Brown shrugged. He was just as confused as I was.

"I can't say, Noob. But the problem's here now. It's got to be fixed right away. Once it's fixed, we can all figure out how it happened in the first place. But the problem's got to be dealt with first. I'll go check out the O2 room. It wouldn't hurt to go down there and check with Green. Maybe I can lend him a helping hand."

"I'll come with you. Maybe Green can use all the help he can get," I said.

Brown shook his head and motioned to the flat screen in front of me.

"You're eager to help and eager to learn. You serve here long enough, and I know you'll have a long and productive career. I appreciate your sentiment, but you've still got some more meteors to clear."

Brown was right, of course. I was far from done. I couldn't just leave my task hanging. If we collided with a meteor, it would be disastrous to say the least. I had to stay and finish what I was doing. Still, something was nagging at me. A feeling that I *had* to go with Brown.

"Are you sure? I mean, you and Green could probably use the help," I said. "I'm not experienced with cutting-edge technology, but I can make pretty good coffee or tea!"

Brown shook his head.

"Thanks for the offer, but I've got this. Just stay here and finish your task."

That was the end of that. I knew Brown well enough by now to know that when he said a discussion was done, it was done. I had to follow his orders. This was nothing like a cat getting stuck in a vent or a dog peeing on the controls.

"All right, I'll just finish this then," I said.

"You do that, Red. Don't worry. This whole thing's probably just a minor malfunction or something. It's probably nothing that a good maintenance check can't fix."

Brown left me there to finish blasting those asteroids to dust. It was still fun. There was no way a task like this couldn't be fun. Blasting asteroids with a high-powered laser never got old. But I still couldn't shake that bad feeling I had at the back of my mind. Something told me that there was more to this than meets the eye.

I ignored the sinking feeling I had and proceeded to blast the remaining meteors until there was nothing left. The screen finally read "Task Cleared," and I was done. Hooray! Normally after completing a game, I would reward myself with chocolate pie, but I had none. Instead, I gave myself a clap.

"There! Now maybe I can go and help Brown," I said to myself.

My terrible nagging feeling was suddenly justified when I heard a cry of pain in the distance. It was a familiar voice. Brown!

I hope it's just a dog having a little pee, I thought.

I dropped the gamepad. In any normal situation, you couldn't pull me away from a gamepad like that. But I heard that terrible cry of agony, and I couldn't just ignore it.

I ran as fast as I could to the O2 room. My heart was beating out of my chest every step of the way. I didn't want to think the worst, but Brown really sounded like he was in pain. What could have happened to him?

It was a short dash to the O2 room. I made it there in no time at all. When I arrived, I came upon a terrible sight. He was on the ground—stabbed in the back. Whoever had done it was long gone.

I just stood there and stared at Brown's body for what seemed like forever. I was in complete shock. A few moments before, he had been alive and well, showing me how to clear meteors. Now, he was lying on the ground, lifeless. I didn't know what to do.

"What happened here?"

I was shaken out of my shock by a familiar voice. It was Green.

"What did you do here, Red? You killed Brown!" I couldn't believe what I was hearing.

"I didn't kill him! I just discovered him like this! He said he was going to check up on you and help you fix the O2 room, and then... and then..."

And then I'd found him dead. It was the truth, but Green wouldn't listen.

Suddenly, this job wasn't so fun anymore.

Red Data Log, Entry #3

The Testy Captain White

The emergency meeting was a disaster to say the least. We went there with the intention of revealing the killer, and instead it turned into a shooting match between Blue and Green. Both of them ended up blasting each other. That wasn't how it was supposed to end.

We all took it pretty hard, but I think Captain White took it the worst. He wasn't the same.

I had known the captain to be someone upbeat and positive. He seemed very hopeful and approachable. Now, he was always uptight.

Every time I saw him, he seemed worried. Even with Green sent away, the captain was always on guard. He was much harder on us all to finish our tasks, too, and was very strict. It was like a new captain had taken over the ship.

"Come on, Red! I need those wires routed and placed on the right nodes, and I need them done now!" Captain White told me earlier.

"I'm on it, Captain White!"

He was working all of us to the bone. I had to take extra tasks that I wasn't really good, at such as defrosting the freezer and opening pickle jars. One of those tasks was making sure all the wires were in their right places in the electrical room. This had been Green's job.

"This is going to be really tough work," I said to myself.

Yellow heard me. "I understand it's tough working in conditions like these, Noob. Care to talk about it?"

As the ship's counselor, Yellow could instantly spot when someone wasn't doing well emotionally. Funny thing is, most of the time, he was pretty stressed out too. Despite that, Yellow's offer to get some of it out of my system sounded good. At that moment, I really could use someone to talk to.

"It's been pretty rough the past few days. I mean, I lost Brown, a good friend and mentor. Then Green and Blue... These days have been pretty rough," I said.

Yellow nodded. His strange alien pet sat on his head as we spoke. It was a little creepy to see a miniature copy of him sitting on his head. Well, at least it usually was. It was funny, but at that moment, I didn't find his pet creepy at all. He suddenly seemed cute and somewhat comforting. Go figure.

"I know what you mean. It's been pretty tough for all of us. It's natural to get stressed out at the events that have come to pass. If you want, you can play with Dave here for a bit."

Yellow handed me his pet alien. Dave seemed to welcome the opportunity to play with me.

"I'd love to, but won't the captain get angry? I mean, I do have to fix the electrical wiring and all."

Yellow shook his head.

"Nah. If he does get on your case, just tell me. I'll be sure to put in a good word for you. Anyway, the captain wouldn't get angry with me!"

"He wouldn't?" I asked skeptically.

"No. I'm the counselor—I know everyone's secrets!"

That was all I needed to hear. I was eager to play with the little guy, and the feeling was mutual. I guess Dave was also getting bored from hanging around Yellow and listening to him rant on and on about his own problems. I could imagine that the little guy wanted a reprieve.

Dave started to tug at my spacesuit playfully. He was human-like, but he sometimes behaved like a little puppy.

For a moment, I felt like all the stress vanished, and I could just enjoy myself.

That moment was cut short when the alarm sounded.

It was a familiar, grating sound, and the lights of the ship blinked on and off. A red hue alternated with darkness all around, and we all realized that power in the ship was starting to fluctuate erratically.

"There's a malfunction in the electrical room!" I said.

"Red! What are you doing here? Didn't I tell you to go down there and fix the wires? If you were doing that, this wouldn't be happening!"

Captain White stormed into the room, and he was furious. I guess I couldn't really blame him. I *was* supposed to be the one doing maintenance work, and he had caught me playing with Dave in the middle of an emergency. Can you blame me, though? Dave is so adorable.

"Oops. Uh, sorry, Captain. I didn't mean to... I mean, I should have... I..."

I got tongue-tied and didn't know what to say.

I thought I was really going to get it, but Yellow stood between us.

"Don't blame the boy, sir. It's my fault. He was going to go down there and check on the wires, but I stopped him. I held him up here and let him play with Dave a bit to ease his stress."

Yellow's voice trembled as he spoke. He was standing up for me, which was a really big thing. Yellow was not a very confrontational person. Unfortunately, he didn't earn anything but the captain's wrath.

"What business do you have teaching Red to slack off, Yellow?" he roared.

"I'm sorry, Captain. I just thought it would be good for him—"

"I'm the captain here! I'm the one who decides things like that!"

We were both surprised at his reaction.

"I'm sorry, sir, but don't forget I know who keeps leaving the toilet seat up!" Yellow said.

Dave crept back to Yellow. He didn't say anything, but he was clearly just as ashamed as Yellow was.

"I heard what happened. You've got to calm down, Captain."

We all turned to see Doc Cross.

"Where have you been, Doc?" the captain asked.

"I was at the med bay just doing maintenance on the equipment there when I heard the discussion here. I make it a point to know what's going on around the ship."

Doc Cross knew that everyone looked up to her as a mother figure of sorts. Next to Brown, she had been the one who was nicest to me. I wasn't surprised that she would try to sort things out.

"Maybe this is the perfect time to just calm down so we can handle the emergencies as they come," she continued. "You said it yourself, Captain. You always told us to remain calm and level-headed in an emergency."

The doc had a lot of guts speaking to Captain White like that. She probably the only one who could speak so candidly to the captain in his current mood.

"I'm calm and collected! Who says I'm not?" the captain said.

"Really? You really think you are? Because if I may speak my mind, sir, I think you're starting to get very uptight. Ever since the incident with Brown, Green and Blue, you haven't really been the same. I understand that it was a tough situation, but we need our calm and collected captain now," Doc Cross said.

Her words seemed to strike a chord with the captain. He paused for a moment.

"I have to take control. I am the captain of this ship!" Captain White said.

"Yes, but perhaps Doctor Cross does have a point," said Pink, arriving in the doorway.

He was also trying to let the Captain see reason. Captain White was still seething.

"I'm not calm? I think I am, and I think I'm doing what's appropriate to handle this and the other emergencies that have plagued us!" the captain said. "Besides, we don't have the time to debate my actions. We still have to deal with *this* emergency!"

The captain was right of course. There was no time to talk when electrical power to the entire ship was going haywire like this. Debates and blame could be saved for later when the emergency was resolved.

Naturally, Pink volunteered to get the job done.

"I'll check it out and see if I can fix the wires," he said.

Pink seemed to be the only one who was not affected by the captain's outburst. He spoke calmly and in his usual logical manner. He knew what had to be done, and he was going to do it.

"I'll come with you, Pink. You might need some help with fixing the wiring," Doc Cross said.

"All right. You two get on it. But hurry up. Every moment the ship's electrical system is malfunctioning like this, we're running the risk of crashing," the captain said.

Yellow turned away from us. He looked really stressed now, pushed to his limit.

"I've got to retreat to my room. Excuse me, everyone, but this is all just too much for me to handle. I'll accept any disciplinary action for what happened with me and Red later. I just need to rest now," he said.

Then everyone was gone, and it was just me and Captain White. I didn't want to be the only one there with the captain in such a foul mood. I thought about maybe defusing the situation by tap-dancing, but it really wasn't the time.

"Captain White, I'm sorry for messing around earlier. I know I should have headed to the electrical room sooner. I..."

The captain raised a hand and shook his head.

"Never mind that now, Red. Just man the bridge and the navigational systems. We can settle everything later."

I went to the bridge and began to check the computers. It was difficult work, especially with the electricity going on and off like that. Somehow I managed, and eventually the power was stabilized.

"They did it! Finally, maybe I can get some work done!" I said.

I was wrong. I wouldn't get any work done. None of us would.

"Help! Someone help!"

We heard the cry of terror coming from the electrical room. It was Pink's voice, and he sounded terrified. The captain and I rushed to the scene.

Pink was standing over the dead body of Doc Cross.

"Help! Someone snuck up from behind me and knocked me out while I was working. When I woke up, I found Doc Cross lying here, dead!"

Pink sounded almost hysterical. There was nothing logical about this situation at all.

The impostor was still among us

Captain White, Data Log Entry #1

The Emergency Meeting

I immediately called the emergency meeting after Green had discovered Brown. He had also found our new crew member, Red, standing suspiciously over Brown's dead body.

As captain of the Gos, I had every authority to call the meeting. There was a lot to discuss here, and tension hung over us all. This is the second death on the ship, if you count the plant that I forgot to water.

Every crew member was present and accounted for. Green sat across from Red, glaring accusatorily. Yellow, our chief counselor, was sitting on the edge of his seat. Yellow has always been something of a nervous wreck. I guess it's because he's always absorbing the crew's emotional problems. His pet alien sat on his head, like it always did. I guess it's better than having a dog sitting on your head all the time. The small human-like alien wore a yellow space suit like his owner and seemed a lot calmer than Yellow.

Yellow said the alien comforted him from the stresses of his job. He was one of the main advocates for our crew members to bring pets on board. Stress came with his job, but he was extra nervous at this meeting, and understandably so.

Pink, our computer systems expert, was sitting quietly beside me. He seemed as cold and calculating as he had always been. Blue, our weapons handler, was sitting beside Pink. His dog was actually on a leash today. Rounding out our tense group was Cross. Cross was the only crew member who wasn't color-coded. She was our team doctor and wore a huge cross on her spacesuit. She was a mother figure of sorts.

"All right. Everyone's present and accounted for. As you all know, I called this emergency meeting to discuss the terrible events that transpired today."

No one spoke, and I continued.

"Green discovered Brown's dead body with Red standing over him. Recent findings also indicate that the oxygen tanks were tampered with, and that caused the alarm. They've been fixed now, but this only further strengthens the terrible conclusion that we've all reached. There's an impostor among us."

No one responded. The tension in the meeting room was heavy.

"I've called this meeting so we can figure out who this impostor is and get rid of him before he causes even more trouble," I finished.

Green pointed at Red and directly accused him. "You want to know who the impostor is? It's pretty simple! It's Red!"

"It's not me! I had no reason to kill Green! I'm no murderer! I mean, I was just doing my task in the meteor room like Brown had asked me to do. Right when I was done, I heard a scream, and I dashed down to the O2 room.

That was when I found Brown lying on the floor, dead," Red said.

Red sounded sincere. And I couldn't see why he *would* kill Green. I mean, like I said, he looked like a big red tomato in his suit, and everyone knows tomatoes are not dangerous.

"I don't think Red did it. He's just a newbie. And he was being trained by Brown. What would Red gain from killing his own mentor?" Pink said.

Among all of us, Pink was the least emotional. He was always trying to figure out or calculate some kind of answer. Even now, in such a tense situation, he didn't seem the least bit nervous. All Pink seemed to care about was who really had done this.

"It's horrible, just horrible! We've got an impostor in our ranks! Someone wants to kill us all!" Yellow said.

Yellow was just being himself. He had always had paranoid ideas about danger lurking about. I felt uneasy around him sometimes. He's always been one of those guys who believes everything he reads on the internet. He once tried to convince me that the Earth was flat!

"Someone wants to kill us all! I knew it was too dangerous to be flying out here in space in the middle of nowhere!" Yellow said. Yellow was on the verge of breaking down. His alien was patting him on the back for comfort. It wasn't working. Yellow was still freaking out. The alien made soothing sounds as well, like a dolphin humming.

"Yellow, just shut up already! If we find out who the killer is, I'm shooting him with my blaster and ending the problem right here and now!" Blue said.

Blue was the complete opposite of Yellow. Blue wasn't afraid of anything and didn't mind facing a threat head on. For Blue, the best solution to any threat was a good laser blast. That was a good reason to have Blue as our weapons specialist. The amusing thing about Blue was that his pet dog, Buddy, was really tiny.

Buddy began to growl. He may have been small, but he was just as feisty as his master. I'm glad he didn't know how to use a gun, otherwise it would have been like a bad roleplay of Han Solo and Chewbacca. The pet was getting agitated and looked ready to pounce on any threat. Maybe he was sniffing out the imposter.

"I'm not sure if Red did it. He's the new kid on the block. He's young and quite harmless," Cross said.

Cross was quite protective of him.

"You're all being fooled by Red's innocent-boy facade!" Green shouted. "He's the one who did it, I know it! Why else would he be there standing over Brown's dead body? I just caught him before he could escape or make it look like he was innocent!"

Green was insisting on Red's guilt. But none of us were buying it. Pink said what was on everyone's mind.

"I don't think he's guilty. I think *you're* the guilty party, Green," Pink said in his usual logical tone.

"Me? *Me*? What are you talking about, Pink? Why would I be the killer?" Green said.

"For starters, you're quick to point fingers at Red. You're a little too eager to accuse him. Perhaps to cover your own guilt?" Pink said.

"I have to agree with Pink," Cross said. "It seems a little fishy that you're so hasty to accuse Red like that. Besides, it's common knowledge around the ship that you didn't like Brown very much. You often thought he was too much of a nice guy, and you once insulted his cooking. You even questioned his position on the ship."

"They didn't get along? I didn't know that. Brown was always so nice and helpful to everyone. Even before he was murdered, he was so eager to help Green," Red said.

"There's a lot of stuff you don't know yet," I told him. "It's tough being on a ship for a long time with the same people. We are like one big dysfunctional family. You have to get along or at least try your best to."

"I have to agree with the captain there, Red. As counselor of the ship, I've had to deal with a lot of the crew members and their disagreements. You would be surprised how often they just don't get along, especially when the toilet seat is left up," Yellow said.

"So who do you think killed Brown?" Red said. Yellow paused before answering.

"I have to say, well, I don't want to jump to conclusions, but..."

"Oh, just spit it out already!" Blue said. Buddy barked in unison with Blue.

"I think it was Green. I mean, he did have that rivalry with Brown that was simmering under the surface. Both of them talked to me about their issues privately, but they never settled it. And Green was always a lot more aggressive than Brown ever was. Oh, sometimes I hate my job! I've always got to absorb everyone's negative emotions on this ship!" Yellow said.

"Yeah, that's why you're always so uptight! Talking about your feelings, calling meetings to discuss who killed who? It's a waste of time, all of it is! If you ask me, the best solution is a good weapon," Blue said.

"We're not here to kill anyone. There's been more than enough of that already. What do you think, Blue? Who do you think killed Brown?" I asked.

Blue shrugged.

"What I think doesn't really matter. I'll leave all the thinking to you all. I just like to blow things up and play with Buddy. Actually, I have an idea!"

Blue picked up Buddy with one hand and walked around the room, letting Buddy sniff every person in turn. Suddenly, he started to bark at Red.

"Aha!" said Blue. "It's Red!"

Red stood up and then placed his hand in his pocket. "It's not me! I have a sausage in my pocket; that's why he's barking!"

"Oh..." said Blue, sounding disappointed. "Can I have it?"

"No!" said Red, sounding offended.

"Okay, never mind. I'll let you guys decide. I'm out!" said Blue.

It was a typical answer from Blue. I wasn't really surprised. But it was becoming pretty clear how this meeting was going.

"Except for Blue, they're all voting against me! What's your vote, Captain White?" Green asked.

His tone was rather desperate. He could see that just about everyone in the meeting was convinced of his guilt. Perhaps Green was hoping I would overrule the majority decision.

I paused a long time before answering. At that moment, I have to admit, I felt like Yellow. There are times I hate this job. As captain of the ship, I always have to be the last line of authority. I always have to maintain order and have the final say in everything. That can get to a person. It can really be stressful, especially in situations like this emergency meeting. I didn't relish any of this, but I had to say my piece.

"I agree with the others. I'm sorry, Green, but I think you killed Brown."

"What? How could you say that, Captain White? I've always been a loyal crew member! I'm no killer! I'm no impostor! I let you borrow my *socks*!"

Green was clearly devastated by my decision.

"Okay, so you made your decision, Captain!

Can I waste Green now?" Blue said.

"You're not wasting anyone, Blue! That's inhumane! We're ejecting Green at intergalactic speed in a cramped pod to be tried for his crime. I've already contacted the proper authorities, and I've programmed an escape pod to head to the nearest space station. It's not too far from here, and it will be a relatively smooth ride, except for the biting spiders. It's a lot better than the fate that Green wanted for us, anyway"

"I *told* you, I'm not the impostor here!"

Green was insisting on his innocence, but I would have none of it. As captain of the Gos, I couldn't show indecision. That would be showing weakness and would promote a lack of faith in me. That would be disastrous, and

I couldn't let it happen. I had made my choice, and I would stick with it.

"I've made up my mind. We've all made our decision here, Green. Just come along quietly, and this will all be done. I'll even give back your socks!" I said.

"No! No way am I getting in that pod! Not when I'm innocent!"

Green stood up, alert and ready for anything. It was pretty clear that he was not going to go quietly.

"Oh, yeah! Gimme a reason to blast you! I'm going to fry you!" Blue said.

Blue pulled out his blaster and pointed it at Green. He was ready to fire. Buddy was snarling now.

This was the perfect opportunity for Blue to use his skills, and I didn't like it at all. I just wanted this to be settled quietly and with little conflict. Looking back, I guess I was pretty naive.

"Oh, no! This is not good. Not good at all! Let's all just settle down and talk about this. We can settle anything as long as we're open with our feelings!" Yellow said.

This was all too much for him to take. The stress and tension was just getting unbearable. I couldn't really blame him. I was getting stressed out too. We all were.

"You're not going to get anywhere with this kind of behavior, Green. Best to just turn yourself in." Pink said, coldly.

"Stand behind me, Red. I'll protect you," Doc Cross said.

Pink was as logical as always and Doc Cross was acting like the protective mother to Red. Everyone was just being themselves, and this was fast turning into chaos. I had to do something to restore order in the ship.

"Don't shoot him, Blue! Look, Green. Just give it up already. No one's going to hurt you. Not here, and not in the space base where the escape pod will take you," I said.

"I didn't do it, Captain White! I didn't! I can't believe you would just let this happen! I'm not the impostor!" Green insisted.

"Just step inside the escape pod already and..."

"I'm not stepping inside anywhere!" Green said. "I *hate* spiders!"

What happened next felt like slow motion. We all watched Green pull out his blaster and aim it at Blue.

"No! Stop it!" I said.

"We don't need to get violent here!" Yellow said.

He hid under the table with his pet alien. The two of them crouched there while Blue and Green shot it out.

They weren't stopping, of course. Blue zapped Green, and Green went flying, but not before managing to take a shot. Blue crumpled to the ground like a soda can crushed under a boot.

"Green! Blue!"

Doc Cross ran toward the men. Neither was moving.

"What happened? Are they all right?" I asked. "This doesn't look good," Pink said.

Doc Cross checked both of them and turned to us. She shook her head. She didn't need to say anything. They were both gone.

"Let's just say you can keep Green's socks!" said Doc Cross.

Two more crewmates were dead, and it all happened on my watch.

I can't help but blame myself for everything that's happened..

Captain White Data Log, Entry #2

The Second Emergency Meeting

Doc Cross was dead. She was found stabbed in the back, lying on the electrical room floor. It was just like what happened to Brown. It only confirmed our worst fears. The impostor was not Green. It was someone else, and that someone was still among us. I felt awful. I was going to put Green in a tiny escape pod with scary biting spiders!

I had no choice but to call another emergency meeting of the remaining crew members.

I took a moment and looked all around me. The empty seats that were supposed to be occupied by Blue, Brown, Green, and Doc Cross were all quite unnerving. Even Buddy, Blue's little dog, had been keeping to Blue's old quarters, only emerging when one of us put down his food.

"As you all know, Doc Cross was found dead, stabbed in the back, just like Brown was. Apparently, the impostor was not Green and has struck again," I said.

"It's Yellow!"

Pink pointed an accusing finger at Yellow. He was really not himself. He was very emotional and was insistent that Yellow had done the deed.

"Me? Why are you pointing the finger at me?" Yellow said, clearly shocked.

"You were the only one who was in your room when the incident happened. The captain and Red were at the bridge, maintaining the ship's course. It would have been easy for you to sneak behind me and knock me out while you killed Doc Cross!" Pink said.

"And why would I do that? I do not like to use violence or even get into any kind of conflict!" Yellow insisted.

"A nice front that you put up to shift the blame. You're the ship's counselor, and you like people running to you for help with their problems. Doc Cross was stealing your limelight!" Pink said.

Yellow shook his head. So did Dave.

"That's just silly! I wasn't jealous of her! *You're* the one with the means and the

55

ability to pull all of this off. You're the one that likes to plot, plan and calculate his every move! I'm sure you're the one who's been doing all this!" Yellow said.

Yellow had a point, of course. Of all of my crew, Pink was always the most focused. He was the one who never let his emotions get in the way. When it came to technical know-how to pull off all that had been plaguing our ship, Pink was a reasonable candidate.

Yet, emotionally, Yellow was quite unstable. All his time being our counselor had really taken its toll on him. He had grown paranoid, tense and stressed from taking in all our worries and troubles. If there was someone I could see with motive to do all of it, it was Yellow. Perhaps he had simply snapped and just lost control.

But Pink also had motive to do all of this. So far, the impostor had targeted two of my biggest supporters, Brown and Doc Cross. The only time I ever saw Pink get slightly emotional was when he questioned my orders. Perhaps he had killed my supporters so he could take over as captain.

Perhaps Pink was planning a mutiny. He definitely had the brains and drive for such a task. Maybe he had always felt that he should have been the captain instead.

I had to weigh all of this and make some kind of a decision. It wouldn't be easy at all.

"I think it was Pink." Red blurted out his vote before I asked.

I guess it wasn't surprising that he would vote against Pink. Yellow was kind and understanding to him. Pink was always cold and distant. Now it was up to me to decide. If I voted against Yellow, it would be a draw, a stalemate. But if I voted for Pink, he would have to go.

"Come on, Captain! You know it's Yellow! All the stress has gotten to him! He's lost his sense of reality!" Pink said. "He knows all of our secrets too!"

"I've lost my *sense of reality*? Just listen to yourself! You're supposed to be the most logical in the crew, the one most like the computers you handle. But are you being logical accusing me like this? Is that logic or emotions gone wild because you want to cover up your crimes so desperately?" Yellow said.

It was a compelling argument from Yellow. And the thought of Pink trying to pull off a mutiny to undermine my authority really seemed to fit. I couldn't let something like that happen, no. I had worked too hard to become a captain to let it all go to waste.

Also, Yellow does know my deepest, darkest secrets, like how I once fell on a chicken and totally flattened it.

"I'm sorry, Pink. I believe you're the impostor."

I spoke plainly and with little emotion. Pink didn't say anything, just stared.

"You're making a big mistake here, Captain," he said.

"No, you're not, Captain. He's the impostor," Yellow said.

I saw Dave sitting on Yellow's head nodding in approval. Red didn't say anything. He seemed as if he just wanted to get everything over with.

"I'm sorry, Pink. This meeting is finished. Please step into the escape pod."

I motioned for Pink to move. I admit, after the fiasco of the first meeting, I expected Pink to make some kind of a move. He didn't.

Pink simply got up from his chair and began to walk toward the escape pod. I followed him, alert just in case he tried something. I had learned my lesson from the last meeting, and I was going to make sure that this all went down without incident.

"I understand you're worried, Captain, but you have nothing to fear. I'm not going to start a riot like Green and Brown did," Pink said calmly.

I guess he was still logical, after all. His sharp mind had sensed my apprehension.

"I'm just making sure, Pink." He nodded.

"I know, Captain. I have to say, once again, you are definitely making a big mistake here. I'm not the impostor. He will strike again."

I didn't say anything. What could I have said? Pink left it at that and stepped inside the escape pod. This one had mosquitoes. In the cramped space, Pink wouldn't even be able to swat them.

"Wait, please, these mosquitoes!" begged Pink.

I decided it was not right. He should at least have a fly swatter in there with him. It just so happens that Doc Cross collects fly swatters like trophies, and I grabbed one and tossed it to Pink.

"But I still can't move in here! It doesn't even— " said Pink, but I cut him off.

"You're welcome, Pink. it was good knowing you!" I said.

We all watched silently as the escape pod was ejected from the Gos like a small bullet fired from a giant gun.

Pink's words stuck in my head. What if he was right? What if we had voted wrong again, and the impostor was still with us? Still among us?

Red Data Log, Entry #4
Skeleton Crew

After Pink left peacefully with all those mosquitoes, a brief period of calm came over the Gos. We were just three crew members now, and the impostor had done a lot of damage.

But everything seemed to go back to normal. Perhaps we had voted the right person. Perhaps it was really over now, and we could resume daily life on the Gos. Even if we were just a skeleton crew, we could make this work. We all had to multi-task now. We all had to share in the responsibilities of maintaining the Gos. Even Dave had some duties now— nothing too hard, just making us tea and coffee.

Captain White wasn't as testy and demanding as before, and he became the old easygoing but reliable captain from before this all happened. We could all approach him again with any concerns we had with no fear of him losing his temper. That made us all work even more efficiently. The work was tough, but it was manageable. With the captain's new attitude and our motivation, we got things done.

Things were starting to look up. Even Yellow was starting to loosen up and not be so nervous all the time. He had actually started to laugh and crack jokes. That was surprising—Yellow had never had a sense of humor before.

Even Dave didn't seem to mind the new jobs that he had to do. For an intelligent alien like Dave, the work was an enjoyable new challenge. It was a welcome change of pace from always trying to cheer up Yellow.

It was actually a welcome change of pace for all of us. We were starting to think that we had gotten past the impostor and all the trouble he had given us.

It was just another one of those days when the captain asked Yellow to check the engine room, which was now one of Yellow's many tasks.

"Yellow get down to the engine room and do some maintenance. Red, go to admin and make sure our records are in order."

We both acknowledged our orders and headed to our respective rooms.

Checking records in the admin room was nothing special. I just checked a lot of records and did a lot of card swiping to make sure everything was in place.

"Where does this go? Does this go here? This is so complicated! I should never have agreed to do this!"

It was Yellow. I heard him talking to himself and complaining from the engine room. The two rooms were pretty close together, so I could easily hear him. I laughed to myself as I heard Yellow muttering. It wasn't surprising. His work was a lot tougher, and I could imagine he would need a while to get the hang of it. After all, he was supposed to be a counselor, not an electrician.

"I'm coming over to help, Yellow!" I called out. "That won't be necessary!" he called back.

I ignored his protest. I was sure that Yellow was just trying to act tough. Well, he wasn't fooling me.

I stepped inside the engine room, and I was shocked at what I saw.

Yellow was hunched over in front of the engine. He was having a lot of trouble attaching what appeared to be explosives on the engine. The explosives were scattered all over the floor, and there were timers on them.

"Yellow, what—what are you doing?" I shouted.

I knew what he was doing, though.

"I told you not to come in here! You just had to barge in! You weren't supposed to see this, Red!" Yellow said.

In a flash, I realized what had happened. We had been wrong all this time. Now, the real impostor was standing right in front of me. There could be no denying it now.

"You're the impostor. You were always the impostor!" I said.

"So now you know. So what? You shouldn't have seen any of this, Red. Now, I'm going to have to kill you then continue my work!"

Yellow pulled out a laser blaster. He pointed it right at me. I raised my hands.

"Whoa, whoa. Don't do this, Yellow. You don't have to do something you're going to regret," I said.

"I *do* have to do this!" Yellow insisted.

In the face of danger, Yellow's answer actually intrigued me.

"You *have* to do this? Why? Why did you kill Brown and Doc Cross? Why did you set up Pink and Green? Why are you doing all of this, Yellow?" I asked.

Yellow paused for a moment, considering the question. It did seem strange. Under all his stress, he always seemed to be a nice person, someone who never agreed with violence. Someone who couldn't hurt a fly.

"You don't understand, Red. I don't want to do this. I *have* to!" Yellow said again.

"You don't have to do any of this, Yellow. Just put the gun down and we can talk about this," I said, trying to not tremble.

Yellow hesitated. For a moment, I thought that I had gotten to him. It was a brief flash of hope that came and went like a shooting star.

"No. I'm sorry, Red."

"But... I can give you anything, Yellow. I have sausages, really tasty ones!"

"I don't like sausages!" said Yellow. It was at this point I realized that maybe Yellow was crazy. Who doesn't like sausages? "I'm sorry!"

Yellow spoke firmly and with no hesitation. He was going to shoot me and resume planting those bombs. I had to do something. I couldn't just let him get away with this. I didn't want to die!

I did the only thing I could think of. I rushed Yellow. I dived like a cannonball right for Yellow's belly. I moved so fast and so suddenly that I surprised him. I tackled him just as he managed to fire the shot. It went wild, missing me by a mile. I pinned him to the floor like a professional wrestler coming out of retirement.

We were on the ground now, rolling around. It was a terrible struggle for Yellow's gun. Total chaos. Yellow couldn't get another shot off, but I couldn't get to his gun either. It was pretty much a stalemate.

"Get off me, Red!" Yellow said. "Give me the gun!" I said.

It probably went on like this for only a few moments, but it felt like an eternity.

The blaster slid away, kicked by one of us in the struggle. Now neither of us could reach it.

I rolled on top of him, raised my fist and punched Yellow in the face, then threw a few more punches. I had the advantage now, and I wasn't going to give it away.

"That's enough, Red!"

I turned around and saw Captain White.

"Captain! I was going to check on the engine like you asked, and I found Red planting bombs all over the engine! I tried to stop him, and he overpowered me!" Yellow said.

I was horrified at Yellow's words. It was the other way around! And now Yellow was trying to twist it around so he could get away. This was a terrible impostor—he would do anything to deflect blame and escape.

This was bad—really bad.

"No, it wasn't like that at all, Captain! I was the one who discovered *Yellow* planting the bombs! I managed to overpower him just now. He's been the impostor all along! We have to get him off this ship!" I pleaded.

The captain just stood there silently, trying to figure us out. If he thought I was the impostor, I was done for, and so was the captain! If I was ejected from the ship, he would be alone with Yellow, who would surely kill him. There was nothing I could do now but wait and hope the captain decided in my favor. For my sake and his.

The captain stood there silently for a long time. Finally, he spoke up.

"Get off of Yellow, Red."

I didn't like the tone of the captain's order. He had decided against me!

"Sir, you're making a big mistake! I'm not the impostor! Yellow is the one who caused all the trouble!"

"I'm glad you've seen the light, Captain! *Red* is the one who caused all the trouble. Now we can eject him, and all the madness will finally end!" Yellow said.

The captain raised a hand, signaling both of us to stop talking. I expected the worst, and Yellow expected the best. This only made what the captain had to say even more surprising.

"Yellow, step away from Red. I'm sending you to the space base for trial for crimes committed as the impostor."

I exhaled. He had made the right choice.

"No! No! You're wrong, Captain! I'm not the impostor; Red is!"

The captain shook his head as he pulled out his own blaster. It was pointed right at Yellow.

"Come quietly, Yellow. It's over. It's really over now."

"No! No! No!"

In a burst of sudden strength, Yellow turned over a nearby table, shielding himself. The captain fired his blaster. The shot destroyed the table, but Yellow was not hurt. He made a break for it.

"You're just making this more difficult for yourself, Yellow!" the captain said.

Yellow turned and ran, and the two of us were right behind him. The captain didn't fire any more shots for fear of hitting some vital machinery along the way. We just both did our best to keep up with Yellow.

He ran as fast as he could. We didn't slow down either. By the time we had cornered him, all three of us were out of breath.

"It's over, Yellow. There's nowhere to run!" the captain said.

"Give it up already, Yellow. Just make it easy for all of us!" I said.

"You're not going to throw me off this ship! I'm not heading into any space base against my will!"

Yellow said.

"You've got no other choice now, Yellow. You're getting into an escape pod, one way or another!" the captain said. "If you come quietly, I can give you a cookie to enjoy on the way to the prison."

Yellow's back was against the wall. I could tell he was contemplating the generous offer of one cookie. Behind him was the sliding panel that led to the escape pods and the vastness of space.

"What *kind* of cookie?" said Yellow.

"Erm.. raisin and oatmeal, the best kind!" said the captain.

"That's *not* the best kind! I would rather just die!"

Suddenly the panel behind Yellow opened. Yellow slipped out of the open panel and was sucked out into the vacuum of space. Well, he had said he'd rather die than eat that cookie.

"Nooooooo!"

That was the last thing we ever heard from Yellow.

"How did that happen? That was not supposed to happen!" the captain said.

"Yes, that was so strange," I said. "It sure was..."

"Oh, and Captain? Raisin and oatmeal *is* the best kind of cookie!"

"Thank you, Red."

He was beside himself and for good reason. The panel door should never have opened unless someone inside the ship activated it. But both of us were here. So who could have done that?

The captain and I both ran to the nearest window. We looked outside into the vast darkness that was space. We saw the small figure of Yellow floating away. There was nothing we could do but watch in shock. And that was when we saw the message suddenly flash out in space, just as Yellow floated away.

YELLOW WAS NOT THE IMPOSTOR.

Red Data Log, Entry #5

The Real Imposter

"Captain, did you just see what I saw out there?" I asked.

I tried to control the fear and confusion in my voice. I just couldn't understand.

"I did, and I can't explain it. That message appeared from out of nowhere. How did that happen?"

Yellow was long gone now. He had disappeared into space, a fate much worse than just being at the space base.

A new message appeared.

I MADE IT HAPPEN. I AM THE REAL IMPOSTOR. THERE IS NO REASON TO HIDE ANYMORE.

The two of us looked at each other. We were the only two crew members on board the ship, and neither of us knew what to make of the strange messages.

The captain finally spoke up.

"Who are you? What's going on?" the captain blurted out.

The impostor displayed his final message. It was straight to the point.

GO TO THE WEAPONS ROOM.

The two of us headed for the weapons room. Neither of us said a word as we raced there. The captain and I knew that this would all be over now, for better or worse. It was time to finally figure out who the impostor really was. We stepped inside the weapons room. There was no one there.

"Where is he? The room is empty!" the captain said.

"I'm right here, just behind storage box A! Can't you see me? Maybe I'm too small. Well, I might as well show myself then."

The small figure jumped out into the open—Dave!

"Dave! It's you? You're the impostor? But how?" the captain said.

Dave cackled evilly.

"You both look surprised. What's wrong? You didn't think that I could be capable of such mayhem? Well, I guess I can't blame you for thinking that. I don't look too threatening," Dave said.

"What's this all about, Dave? How did you do all of this, and why?" I asked.

"You think it was easy being that fool Yellow's pet? I never wanted to be domesticated like this. I never wanted to leave my home planet. Yellow brought me here against my will, changing my life forever. I was once just a quiet and peaceful shapeshifter, like all of us on my planet. When Yellow took me here, he uprooted me from my home, from where I was born. He turned me into his pet even though I didn't want it! But that was the thing that Yellow didn't understand. The thing that none of you understood. I'm no helpless little alien like you think. I have a power that you can't imagine."

Anger was burning inside him. This was not the Dave we all thought we knew. This was someone darker, someone who wanted to hurt us all.

"What is that power, Dave?" I asked.

"Our people have the power to induce stress and worry in other people's minds. It's in the chemicals we release as a natural part of our bodily processes. The chemicals are harmless to us, but to other creatures, including you humans, it can induce extreme worry."

Dave's words explained a lot—why Yellow was always so uptight, for one. Since he was always exposed to Dave, it was no wonder that he was a nervous wreck.

"Well, that explains a lot," the captain said.

"A lot? It explains everything! Do you know what it feels like to be viewed as nothing but a pet? As an oddity after being taken away from your home? Do you think that's fun? Well, that's where all of you made your big mistake! You all underestimated my abilities. I've managed to turn you all against each other without even raising suspicion. And now, the two of you are finally going to die, and my revenge will be complete!"

Dave's words were chilling. This was one pet who wasn't messing around. The captain and I stood there, ready for anything.

Then the captain turned on me and fired his blaster. I was so close that he could not miss. The shot struck me on the shoulder, and the impact sent me flying. I was lying on the ground, clutching my shoulder, when I looked up and saw the captain approaching me. He wasn't hesitating, and he still pointed the blaster at me.

"You're the impostor, Red! You're the impostor, and I'm getting rid of you once and for all!" he said.

The captain's words were clearly not his. I realized what was happening. Dave had said that he could generate stress and anxiety in other beings. It was clear to me that he was generating so much anxiety in the captain that he didn't even recognize me anymore. The captain didn't know what he was doing.

"Captain White! Dave's controlling you! You've got to fight it!" I said.

It was no good. The captain fired. I barely managed to roll out of the way. Perhaps the captain was already fighting Dave's efforts to control him. Maybe that was the reason he'd only injured me earlier and missed his shot now. Perhaps somewhere deep down, it was still Captain White.

"Captain! Fight it, please! You don't know what you're doing!" I said.

"Shut up, Red! You're the impostor, and you're going down!"

He fired again, and I barely managed to dodge his shot. I grabbed a blaster from the wall behind me. I thought about using it, but I couldn't. This wasn't Captain White's fault. He was under Dave's control. I couldn't just shoot him!

Unfortunately, the captain didn't have any such qualms about shooting at me. He fired several more shots that I managed to dodge. I didn't know how long I could keep this up.

"Come on, Captain White! Hit him already! What kind of captain can't shoot straight?" Dave said.

He was getting frustrated that the captain wasn't hitting me. This was all like some crazy movie for Dave, and he was just sitting back and enjoying it while the captain was trying to blow my brains out.

I knew what I had to do. If Dave was controlling the captain, perhaps if I took out Dave, the captain would be able to think a little more clearly.

I fired my blaster at Dave. Unfortunately, I missed. The shot was close, but he managed to dodge it in time. He also realized what I was trying to do.

"He's trying to kill me! You've got to kill him first!" Dave said.

The captain kept firing at me, but somehow, I managed to keep one step ahead of his blasts. Unfortunately, Dave was also dodging mine. This was getting crazy. I realized that we couldn't keep this up forever.

I had to end this, and it had to end now. I saw my chance.

I fired and struck Dave squarely. He went down hard. It was over. It had to be.

"Captain! It's done. Dave was the impostor, and he's done for!" I said.

But the captain didn't know that it was over. He kept firing at me.

"Whoa! Stop it already!"

"You're the impostor, Red! You're going down!"

The only possible explanation for this was that it probably took time before the effects of Dave's stress powers wore off. I didn't know if I could last. The captain seemed to be completely losing it now.

"Captain, snap out of it! Please! Think about cookies!!"

The captain wasn't listening. His shots were getting closer and closer. I was starting to get tired dodging all his shots. Finally, one of them struck me in the same sore shoulder that he'd hit before. The pain was too much. I dropped my gun and fell to the floor.

I looked up and saw the captain point his blaster at me. I closed my eyes and prepared for the worst.

But the captain dropped his gun and stretched his hand out to me.

"Red, I'm sorry..."

"Oh, thank goodness, I thought I was done for!"

"I am remembering now..." "You remember me?"

"No, no. Raisins... and... oatmeal... cookies, the best, are the best!"

It was truly over now.

Captain White Data Log, Entry #3

The End of the Impostor

When I snapped out of Dave's stress-inducing influence, it felt like a cloud had lifted from my eyes. I could see everything more clearly now, and I was finally myself again. I had come close to killing Red, but thankfully the effect wore off just in time. I later realized that Red had killed him.

We shot Dave's body from the ship through the panel Yellow had been sucked through.

We knew we couldn't keep Dave on the ship for many reasons. The most pressing reason was that perhaps his body still generated power. We couldn't risk it. Truth be told, both of us had had enough. We were the only two survivors.

Dave's body floated away into space. Red and I looked on as it slowly drifted away from us. I couldn't help but see the words in my mind as he floated away.

"Dave was the impostor."

Dave finally vanished from our view. It was like he had been swallowed up by space itself. When it was done, Red and I didn't say anything for the longest time. Finally, Red spoke.

"What now, Captain? What do we do now? We're the only two members of the crew left," he said.

It was a good question. We couldn't possibly maintain the ship now. Two people just weren't enough to keep a ship like the Gos going.

"Well, we can't just multi-task anymore. We would simply be overwhelmed. I guess we send a distress call to the nearest space base. They can pick us up from there."

"So we're going home?" Red said. "We're going home," I confirmed. It was finally over.

We hope you had as much fun reading this adventure as we had writing it!

The journey doesn't end here — follow Red and his fellow crewmates on more exciting imposter adventure stories in the Diary of a Crewmate series.

See you in the next book!

Printed in Dunstable, United Kingdom